Intellectual Properties, Trademarks and Copyrights

Contents of this book are fully copyrighted.

Exam topics

As a partnership between the federal government and provinces and territories responsible for apprenticeship training and trade certification in their jurisdictions, the Red Seal Program sets common standards to assess the skills of tradespeople across Canada. Those tradespersons who have successfully passed the Red Seal examination will receive a Red Seal endorsement on their provincial/territorial trade certificate.

Hairstylists shampoo, cut, style and chemically treat hair. They may also provide services such as scalp treatments, hair addition applications and barbering techniques. Hairstylists may work in hair salons, spas, barber shops, schools, hair replacement clinics, health care establishments, hotels, and in the tourism, fashion and entertainment industries

We create these self-practice test questions module referencing the concepts and principles currently valid in the exam. Each question comes with an answer and a short explanation which aids you in seeking further study information. For purpose of exam readiness drilling, this product includes questions that have varying numbers of choices. Some have 2 while some have 5 or 6. We want to make sure these questions are tough enough to really test your readiness and draw your focus to the weak areas. Think of these as challenges presented to you so to assess your comprehension of the subject matters. The goal is to reinforce learning, to validate successful transference of knowledge and to identify areas of weakness that require remediation.

What is the typical cellular arrangement of cocci bacteria?

a. Chains

b. Clusters

c. Pairs

d. Spirals

e. None of these.

Answer: b. Clusters

Explanation: Cocci bacteria typically arrange themselves in clusters.

Streptococci bacteria are characterized by their arrangement in:

a. Pairs

b. Chains

c. Clusters

d. Singles

e. None of these.

Answer: b. Chains

Explanation: Streptococci bacteria are known for forming chains of cells.

Which of the following bacteria is commonly found in pairs?

a. Cocci

b. Streptococci

[c. Diplococci

d. Spirilla

Answer: c. Diplococci

Explanation: Diplococci bacteria typically arrange themselves in pairs.

Spirilla bacteria are characterized by their shape, which is:

a. Round

b. Rod-shaped

c. Spiral

d. Cuboidal

Answer: c. Spiral

Explanation: Spirilla bacteria have a spiral or helical shape.

Which bacterial structure is responsible for the movement of spirilla bacteria?

a. Flagella

b. Pili

c. Capsule

d. Cell wall

e. None of these.

Answer: a. Flagella

Explanation: Flagella are responsible for the movement of spirilla bacteria.

Cocci bacteria are generally classified based on their:

a. Size

b. Color

c. Arrangement

d. Motility

Answer: c. Arrangement

Explanation: Cocci bacteria are often classified based on their arrangement.

Streptococci bacteria are commonly associated with infections in the:

a. Respiratory system

b. Digestive system

c. Urinary system

d. Nervous system

e. None of these.

Answer: a. Respiratory system

Explanation: Streptococci are often associated with respiratory infections.

Diplococci bacteria are often responsible for causing infections in the:

a. Skin

b. Genitourinary system

c. Digestive system

d. Cardiovascular system

Answer: b. Genitourinary system

Explanation: Diplococci are commonly associated with infections in the genitourinary system.

The protoplasm of a bacterial cell consists of:

a. Nucleus

b. Nucleoid

c. Mitochondria

d. Endoplasmic reticulum

e. None of these.

Answer: b. Nucleoid

Explanation: In bacteria, the genetic material is found in the nucleoid region, not within a true nucleus.

What is the primary function of the bacterial cell wall, which is absent in animal cells?

a. Protection

b. DNA replication

c. Energy production

d. Protein synthesis

Answer: a. Protection

Explanation: The bacterial cell wall provides structural support and protection to the bacterial cell, a feature absent in animal cells.

Binary fission is a reproductive process commonly observed in:

a. Plants

b. Bacteria

c. Animals

d. Fungi

Answer: b. Bacteria

Explanation: Binary fission is the method of reproduction in bacteria where a single cell divides into two identical daughter cells.

Pediculosis capitis refers to an infestation caused by:

a. Fleas

b. Ticks

c. Lice

d. Mites

e. a and b

Answer: c. Lice

Explanation: Pediculosis capitis is a medical term for a head lice infestation.

Hepatitis B is primarily transmitted through:

a. Airborne droplets

b. Contaminated water

c. Sexual contact

d. Mosquito bites

e. a and b

Answer: c. Sexual contact

Explanation: Hepatitis B is a viral infection that is commonly transmitted through unprotected sexual contact and exposure to infected blood or other bodily fluids.

Which of the following microorganisms is responsible for the fermentation process in yogurt production?

a. Escherichia coli

b. Saccharomyces cerevisiae

c. Lactobacillus bulgaricus

d. Staphylococcus aureus

Answer: c. Lactobacillus bulgaricus

Explanation: Lactobacillus bulgaricus is a bacterium used in the fermentation of yogurt.

What is the main method of reproduction in bacteria like Escherichia coli?

a. Binary fission

b. Budding

c. Conjugation

d. Spore formation

Answer: a. Binary fission

Explanation: Escherichia coli reproduces primarily through binary fission.

Pediculosis capitis is commonly known as:

a. Ringworm

b. Head lice

c. Scabies

d. Bedbugs

Answer: b. Head lice

Explanation: Pediculosis capitis is the medical term for an infestation of head lice.

Hepatitis B can lead to chronic liver disease and increase the risk of:

a. Lung cancer

b. Kidney failure

c. Heart disease

d. Liver cancer

Answer: d. Liver cancer

Explanation: Chronic infection with Hepatitis B can lead to liver cirrhosis and an increased risk of liver cancer.

Which of the following is NOT a characteristic of microorganisms?

a. They are unicellular

b. They can be either prokaryotic or eukaryotic

c. They are always harmful to humans

d. They can be beneficial in various processes

Answer: c. They are always harmful to humans

Explanation: Microorganisms can be both harmful and beneficial; many are essential for various processes, such as digestion and fermentation.

The primary purpose of binary fission in bacteria is:

a. Genetic recombination

b. Growth and multiplication

c. Spore formation

d. Budding

Answer: b. Growth and multiplication

Explanation: Binary fission allows bacteria to rapidly multiply and increase their population.

What is the primary function of the nucleus in a cell?

a. Energy production

b. Cellular respiration

c. DNA storage and control

d. Protein synthesis

Answer: c. DNA storage and control

Explanation: The nucleus of a cell contains the genetic material (DNA. and is responsible for controlling cellular activities, including protein synthesis.

What is the primary function of the cytoplasm in a cell?

a. Storage of genetic material

b. Cellular communication

c. Energy production

d. Support and transport of cellular materials

Answer: d. Support and transport of cellular materials

Explanation: The cytoplasm provides structural support and acts as a medium for the movement of cellular components, facilitating various cellular processes.

Which skin layer is primarily responsible for the formation of fingerprints?

a. Epidermis

b. Dermis

c. Hypodermis

d. Papillary layer

Answer: d. Papillary layer

Explanation: The papillary layer of the dermis is responsible for the formation of fingerprints, as it contains ridges and dermal papillae that protrude into the epidermis.

What is the most common cause of Folliculitis barbae?

a. Fungal infection

b. Bacterial infection

c. Viral infection

d. Parasitic infestation

Answer: b. Bacterial infection

Explanation: Folliculitis barbae is typically caused by a bacterial infection of the hair follicles, often resulting from shaving or other forms of hair removal.

What is the function of the nucleolus within the nucleus?

a. Synthesizing lipids

b. Producing ribosomes

c. Storing DNA

d. Controlling cellular respiration

Answer: b. Producing ribosomes

Explanation: The nucleolus is involved in the production of ribosomes, essential cellular structures involved in protein synthesis.

Which part of a cell is responsible for cellular respiration and energy production?

a. Nucleus

b. Mitochondria

c. Endoplasmic reticulum

d. Golgi apparatus

Answer: b. Mitochondria

Explanation: Mitochondria are the cellular organelles responsible for cellular respiration, generating energy in the form of ATP.

What is the medical term for head lice infestation?

a. Pediculosis capitis

b. Scabies capitis

c. Dermatophytosis capitis

d. Tinea capitis

Answer: a. Pediculosis capitis

Explanation: Pediculosis capitis refers to an infestation of head lice, a common parasitic condition affecting the scalp and hair.

Which organelle is responsible for the synthesis and modification of proteins in a cell?

a. Nucleus

b. Golgi apparatus

c. Endoplasmic reticulum

d. Lysosome

e. c and d

Answer: c. Endoplasmic reticulum

Explanation: The endoplasmic reticulum is involved in the synthesis and modification of proteins before they are transported to other cellular locations.

What is the main function of the hypodermis layer in the skin?

a. Temperature regulation

b. Cushioning and insulation

c. Production of melanin

d. Formation of hair follicles

e. c and d

Answer: b. Cushioning and insulation

Explanation: The hypodermis layer serves as a layer of cushioning and insulation, providing support and protection to the underlying tissues.

Which skin layer contains melanocytes responsible for skin pigmentation?

a. Epidermis

b. Dermis

c. Hypodermis

d. Stratum corneum

Answer: a. Epidermis

Explanation: Melanocytes, responsible for skin pigmentation, are primarily found in the epidermis.

What is the role of the Golgi apparatus in a cell?

a. Energy production

b. Protein synthesis

c. Packaging and modification of cellular products

d. Cellular respiration

Answer: c. Packaging and modification of cellular products

Explanation: The Golgi apparatus is involved in packaging and modifying cellular products before they are transported to their final destinations.

What is the primary function of the stratum corneum in the epidermis?

a. Melanin production

b. Cellular division

c. Protection and barrier function

d. Blood vessel formation

Answer: c. Protection and barrier function

Explanation: The stratum corneum is the outermost layer of the epidermis and functions as a protective barrier, preventing dehydration and protecting against external pathogens.

What is the outermost layer of the skin responsible for providing a protective barrier?

a. Dermis

b. Hypodermis

c. Epidermis

d. Papillary layer

Answer: c. Epidermis

Explanation: The epidermis is the outermost layer of the skin and serves as a protective barrier against environmental factors.

In which layer of the skin are melanocytes primarily located, contributing to skin pigmentation?

a. Dermis

b. Epidermis

c. Hypodermis

d. Stratum corneum

Answer: b. Epidermis

Explanation: Melanocytes, responsible for skin pigmentation, are primarily located in the epidermis.

What are the small, often overlapping, structures that cover the skin of certain animals, providing protection and aiding in movement?

a. Fur

b. Scales

c. Feathers

d. Fins

Answer: b. Scales

Explanation: Scales are external structures covering the skin of reptiles, fish, and certain other animals, providing protection and aiding in movement.

What genetic condition is characterized by the absence or lack of pigment in the skin, hair, and eyes?

a. Melanoma

b. Vitiligo

c. Albinism

d. Psoriasis

e. a and b

Answer: c. Albinism

Explanation: Albinism is a genetic condition characterized by the absence or lack of pigment in the skin, hair, and eyes.

What is the central, soft, and often unstructured region found in certain types of hair or feathers?

a. Cortex

b. Cuticle

c. Medulla

d. Follicle

Answer: c. Medulla

Explanation: The medulla is the central, soft, and often unstructured region found in certain types of hair or feathers.

In cosmetology, what is the term for the practice of cleansing and beautifying the skin, hair, and nails?

a. Dermatology

b. Esthetics

c. Trichology

d. Cosmetology

Answer: d. Cosmetology

Explanation: Cosmetology is the practice of cleansing and beautifying the skin, hair, and nails.

Which layer of the epidermis is responsible for the constant renewal of skin cells through cell division?

a. Stratum basale

b. Stratum spinosum

c. Stratum granulosum

d. Stratum corneum

Answer: a. Stratum basale

Explanation: The stratum basale is the deepest layer of the epidermis and is responsible for the constant renewal of skin cells through cell division.

What is the name of the outermost layer of the hair shaft, consisting of overlapping, flattened cells?

a. Cortex

b. Cuticle

c. Medulla

d. Follicle

Answer: b. Cuticle

Explanation: The cuticle is the outermost layer of the hair shaft, consisting of overlapping, flattened cells that provide protection.

Which skin condition is characterized by patches of depigmented skin due to the loss of melanocytes?

a. Albinism

b. Vitiligo

c. Eczema

d. Dermatitis

Answer: b. Vitiligo

Explanation: Vitiligo is a skin condition characterized by patches of depigmented skin due to the loss of melanocytes.

What is the term for the study and treatment of the hair and scalp?

a. Cosmetology

b. Trichology

c. Dermatology

d. Esthetics

Answer: b. Trichology

Explanation: Trichology is the branch of cosmetology that focuses on the study and treatment of the hair and scalp.

Which layer of the epidermis contains cells that are flattened, filled with keratin, and eventually slough off as dead skin cells?

a. Stratum basale

b. Stratum spinosum

c. Stratum granulosum

d. Stratum corneum

Answer: d. Stratum corneum

Explanation: The stratum corneum is the outermost layer of the epidermis, containing flattened, keratin-filled cells that eventually slough off as dead skin cells.

What is the primary function of the sebaceous glands in the skin?

a. Producing sweat

b. Producing melanin

c. Producing oil (sebum) for skin lubrication

d. Producing collagen for skin elasticity

e. None of these.

Answer: c. Producing oil (sebum) for skin lubrication

Explanation: Sebaceous glands produce oil (sebum) to lubricate the skin, preventing it from drying out and contributing to skin health.

What is the structure that surrounds the hair root and is responsible for producing and nourishing the hair strand?

a. Hair shaft

b. Sebaceous gland

c. Hair follicle

d. Medulla

Answer: c. Hair follicle

Explanation: The hair follicle surrounds the hair root and is responsible for producing and nourishing the hair strand.

What is the name of the tiny muscle attached to the hair follicle responsible for causing hair to stand on end (goosebumps)?

a. Sebaceous muscle

b. Dermal muscle

c. Arrector pili muscle

d. Follicular muscle

e. None of these.

Answer: c. Arrector pili muscle

Explanation: The arrector pili muscle is responsible for causing hair to stand on end when contracted, creating goosebumps.

In the formation of proteins, what type of bond links amino acids together?

a. Hydrogen bond

b. Ionic bond

c. Covalent bond

d. Peptide bond

Answer: d. Peptide bond

Explanation: Peptide bonds are covalent bonds that link amino acids together in the formation of proteins.

What term is used to describe the natural pigments that give color to the skin, hair, and eyes?

a. Melanin

b. Carotene

c. Hemoglobin

d. Keratin

Answer: a. Melanin

Explanation: Melanin is the natural pigment responsible for skin, hair, and eye color.

In the context of cosmetics, what are "quantities"?

a. Makeup brushes

b. Measured amounts of product

c. Cosmetic containers

d. Beauty salons

Answer: b. Measured amounts of product

Explanation: In cosmetics, "quantities" refer to measured amounts of product used in various applications.

What is the primary function of the arrector pili muscle in humans?

a. Regulating body temperature

b. Causing hair to stand on end

c. Producing sweat

d. Enhancing blood circulation

e. None of these.

Answer: b. Causing hair to stand on end

Explanation: The arrector pili muscle contracts to cause hair to stand on end, a response known as piloerection or goosebumps.

What is the term for the process by which amino acids are joined together to form a protein chain?

a. Condensation

b. Hydrolysis

c. Peptidation

d. Polymerization

Answer: a. Condensation

Explanation: In the process of protein synthesis, amino acids are joined together through a condensation reaction to form a protein chain.

What is the medical term for dandruff, a common condition characterized by the flaking of the scalp skin?

a. Psoriasis

b. Dermatitis

c. Pityriasis

d. Eczema

Answer: c. Pityriasis

Explanation: Pityriasis is a medical term that includes various skin conditions, and in this context, it refers to dandruff.

Which of the following is NOT a primary color of melanin responsible for red and yellow hues in hair?

a. Eumelanin

b. Pheomelanin

c. Neuromelanin

d. Trichomelanin

Answer: c. Neuromelanin

Explanation: Neuromelanin is a type of melanin found in the brain, and it is not responsible for the coloration of hair.

What is the name of the process by which hair color is changed through the application of chemical substances?

a. Perming

b. Bleaching

c. Coloring

d. Relaxing

Answer: c. Coloring

Explanation: Coloring is the process of changing hair color through the application of chemical substances, such as hair dyes.

What is the primary purpose of the sebaceous glands associated with hair follicles?

a. Producing sweat

b. Regulating body temperature

c. Lubricating the hair and skin

d. Enhancing blood circulation

Answer: c. Lubricating the hair and skin

Explanation: Sebaceous glands produce sebum, an oil that lubricates the hair and skin, preventing dryness.

During which phase of the hair cycle does hair actively grow and cells divide rapidly at the root of the hair follicle?

a. Telogen phase

b. Anagen phase

c. Catagen phase

d. Exogen phase

Answer: b. Anagen phase

Explanation: The anagen phase is the growth phase of the hair cycle, during which cells divide rapidly at the root, leading to active hair growth.

What characterizes the catagen phase of the hair cycle?

a. Active hair growth

b. Hair shedding

c. Transitional phase

d. Resting phase

Answer: c. Transitional phase

Explanation: The catagen phase is a transitional phase between active growth (anagen) and rest (telogen) in the hair cycle.

How long does the anagen phase typically last in the hair cycle?

a. A few days

b. Several weeks to months

c. Several months to years

d. Indefinitely

Answer: c. Several months to years

Explanation: The anagen phase can last for varying durations, ranging from several weeks to several months or even years, depending on factors such as genetics and body location.

What phase of the hair cycle is characterized by the detachment and shedding of the hair strand from the follicle?

a. Anagen phase

b. Telogen phase

c. Catagen phase

d. Exogen phase

e. None of these.

Answer: d. Exogen phase

Explanation: The exogen phase is the shedding phase of the hair cycle, during which the hair strand detaches and falls out.

What factors can influence the duration of the anagen phase in the hair cycle?

a. Diet and exercise

b. Genetics and age

c. Hair care products

d. Environmental pollution

Answer: b. Genetics and age

Explanation: The duration of the anagen phase is influenced by genetic factors and age. Some individuals may naturally have longer or shorter anagen phases.

What percentage of scalp hairs is typically in the telogen phase at any given time in the hair cycle?

a. 5-10%

b. 20-30%

c. 40-50%

d. 60-70%

e. 70-80%

Answer: c. 40-50%

Explanation: Approximately 40-50% of scalp hairs are typically in the telogen phase at any given time, representing hairs in the resting phase of the hair cycle.

What type of chemical bond links amino acids together in the formation of proteins?

a. Ionic bond

b. Hydrogen bond

c. Covalent bond

d. Peptide bond

e. None of these.

Answer: d. Peptide bond

Explanation: Peptide bonds are covalent bonds that link amino acids together to form the backbone of proteins.

In the field of cosmetics, what does the term "quantities" refer to?

a. Makeup application techniques

b. Measured amounts of product

c. Cosmetic brands

d. Beauty salon services

Answer: b. Measured amounts of product

Explanation: In cosmetics, "quantities" refer to measured amounts of product used in various applications.

What is the medical term for dandruff, a common condition characterized by the flaking of the scalp skin?

a. Psoriasis

b. Dermatitis

c. Pityriasis

d. Eczema

Answer: c. Pityriasis

Explanation: Pityriasis is a medical term that includes various skin conditions, and in this context, it refers to dandruff.

What is hypertrichosis?

a. Excessive hair growth

b. Hair loss

c. Normal hair growth

d. Gray hair

e. None of these.

Answer: a. Excessive hair growth

Explanation: Hypertrichosis is a condition characterized by excessive hair growth on areas of the body where terminal hair does not normally grow.

Which of the following is NOT a primary color of melanin responsible for red and yellow hues in hair?

a. Eumelanin

b. Pheomelanin

c. Neuromelanin

d. Trichomelanin

Answer: c. Neuromelanin

Explanation: Neuromelanin is a type of melanin found in the brain and is not responsible for the coloration of hair.

What is the primary factor that contributes to the development of hypertrichosis?

a. Aging

b. Genetics

c. Sun exposure

d. Hormonal changes

e. None of these.

Answer: b. Genetics

Explanation: Genetics is the primary factor contributing to the development of hypertrichosis. It can be congenital or acquired and is often familial.

What is the primary purpose of curl reforming in hairstyling?

a. Creating permanent waves

b. Straightening natural curls

c. Adding volume to hair

d. Enhancing hair color

Answer: b. Straightening natural curls

Explanation: Curl reforming is a hairstyling technique designed to alter the natural curl pattern of the hair, providing a straighter appearance.

In hair coloring, what does "half off-base placement" refer to?

a. Applying color to the entire hair strand

b. Placing foils halfway up the hair shaft

c. Lifting hair color from the roots

d. Coloring the hair at a 45-degree angle

Answer: a. Applying color to the entire hair strand

Explanation: Half off-base placement involves applying color to the entire hair strand, resulting in even color distribution.

What is the primary characteristic of a croquignole perm wrap in hair perming?

a. Vertical sectioning

b. Horizontal sectioning

c. Diagonal sectioning

d. Zigzag sectioning

Answer: b. Horizontal sectioning

Explanation: Croquignole perm wrap involves winding hair horizontally around the perm rod, creating a spiral effect.

What does a spiral wrap technique in hair perming involve?

a. Winding hair vertically around the perm rod

b. Winding hair horizontally around the perm rod

c. Alternating horizontal and vertical winding

d. Wrapping hair in a zigzag pattern

Answer: a. Winding hair vertically around the perm rod

Explanation: In a spiral wrap, hair is wound vertically around the perm rod, creating a spiral curl pattern.

What is the purpose of half off-base placement in hair coloring?

a. Achieving a natural root regrowth look

b. Creating volume at the roots

c. Reducing hair color intensity

d. Adding highlights to the ends

Answer: b. Creating volume at the roots

Explanation: Half off-base placement in hair coloring is used to create volume at the roots, especially in highlighting techniques.

What is the primary benefit of a croquignole perm wrap in perming?

a. Loose, natural-looking curls

b. Defined, tight curls

c. Voluminous, bouncy curls

d. Zigzag-patterned curls

Answer: b. Defined, tight curls

Explanation: Croquignole perm wrap tends to produce defined, tight curls due to the horizontal winding around the perm rod.

In spiral wrap perming, what effect does vertical winding of hair around the rod create?

a. Loose waves

b. Defined curls

c. Volume at the roots

d. Zigzag pattern

Answer: b. Defined curls

Explanation: Vertical winding in spiral wrap perming creates defined curls that cascade down the hair.

What is the primary characteristic of a zigzag sectioning pattern in hair perming?

a. Alternating horizontal and vertical winding

b. Diagonal winding around the perm rod

c. Winding hair in a crisscross pattern

d. Creating uneven curls with varying lengths

Answer: c. Winding hair in a crisscross pattern

Explanation: Zigzag sectioning involves winding hair in a crisscross pattern, resulting in curls with an uneven, natural appearance.

What is a key characteristic of acid-balanced waves in the context of hair perming?

a. High pH levels

b. Harsh chemical composition

c. Low pH levels

d. Strong ammonia scent

Answer: c. Low pH levels

Explanation: Acid-balanced waves have a low pH, which is less harsh on the hair and provides a milder perming effect.

What is a distinguishing feature of no mix-no lye relaxers in hair straightening?

a. Require mixing before application

b. Contain lye (sodium hydroxide)

c. Can be applied directly without mixing

d. Suitable for all hair types

Answer: c. Can be applied directly without mixing

Explanation: No mix-no lye relaxers come pre-formulated and can be applied directly to the hair without the need for mixing with an activator.

What is the primary chemical compound found in lithium hydroxide relaxers?

a. Sodium hydroxide

b. Calcium hydroxide

c. Lithium hydroxide

d. Potassium hydroxide

Answer: c. Lithium hydroxide

Explanation: Lithium hydroxide is the primary chemical compound in relaxers designed for fine or delicate hair.

What distinguishes potassium hydroxide relaxers from sodium hydroxide relaxers?

a. Lower pH levels

b. Stronger chemical composition

c. Gentler on the scalp

d. Faster processing time

Answer: a. Lower pH levels

Explanation: Potassium hydroxide relaxers typically have a lower pH, making them milder and suitable for sensitive scalps.

What defines True acid waves in the context of hair perming?

a. High pH levels

b. Require heat for activation

c. Contain lye (sodium hydroxide)

d. Low pH levels

Answer: d. Low pH levels

Explanation: True acid waves have a low pH, making them gentle on the hair and suitable for fine or color-treated hair.

What is the primary advantage of ammonia-free waves in hair perming?

a. Faster processing time

b. Intense curl formation

c. Reduced odor and scalp irritation

d. Long-lasting results

Answer: c. Reduced odor and scalp irritation

Explanation: Ammonia-free waves are known for having a milder scent and causing less scalp irritation compared to ammonia-containing formulations.

Which type of relaxer is generally recommended for use on fine or color-treated hair due to its milder formulation?

a. Sodium hydroxide relaxer

b. Lithium hydroxide relaxer

c. No mix-no lye relaxer

d. Potassium hydroxide relaxer

Answer: b. Lithium hydroxide relaxer

Explanation: Lithium hydroxide relaxers are often recommended for fine or color-treated hair due to their milder formulation.

What is the primary disadvantage of sodium hydroxide relaxers in comparison to other types?

a. Harsh chemical composition

b. Longer processing time

c. Incompatibility with color-treated hair

d. Limited availability in the market

Answer: a. Harsh chemical composition

Explanation: Sodium hydroxide relaxers are known for their strong chemical composition, which can be harsh on the hair and scalp.

Which relaxer type is suitable for clients who desire a straighter hair texture without excessive curl reduction?

a. Sodium hydroxide relaxer

b. Ammonia-free wave

c. Potassium hydroxide relaxer

d. True acid wave

Answer: c. Potassium hydroxide relaxer

Explanation: Potassium hydroxide relaxers are milder and provide a straightening effect without excessive curl reduction.

In the context of hair perming, what is the purpose of an activator?

a. Provide color to the hair

b. Activate the relaxing agent

c. Neutralize the perm solution

d. Increase processing time

Answer: b. Activate the relaxing agent

Explanation: An activator is used to activate the relaxing agent in relaxer formulations, initiating the chemical process.

Which relaxer type is known for its suitability on resistant hair textures and efficient straightening capabilities?

a. Sodium hydroxide relaxer

b. Lithium hydroxide relaxer

c. No mix-no lye relaxer

d. Ammonia-free wave

Answer: a. Sodium hydroxide relaxer

Explanation: Sodium hydroxide relaxers are often chosen for their effectiveness on resistant hair textures and efficient straightening capabilities.

What precaution should be taken when using True acid waves on color-treated hair?

a. Avoid using color-treated hair

b. Increase processing time

c. Neutralize the perm solution

d. Perform a strand test

Answer: d. Perform a strand test

Explanation: Before using True acid waves on color-treated hair, it's advisable to perform a strand test to ensure compatibility and avoid undesirable results.

Which of the following is a common ingredient found in chemical relaxers used for hair straightening?

a. Olive oil

b. Hydrogen peroxide

c. Sodium hydroxide

d. Aloe vera

Answer: c. Sodium hydroxide

Explanation: Sodium hydroxide is a chemical commonly used in relaxers for its strong straightening effect.

What is the primary purpose of a flat iron in hair straightening?

a. Adding volume

b. Curling hair

c. Removing split ends

d. Applying hair color

Answer: b. Curling hair

Explanation: A flat iron is primarily used for straightening hair, but it can also be used to curl the hair by wrapping sections around the iron.

What is the key benefit of using keratin treatments for hair straightening?

a. Temporary straightening effect

b. Intense curl formation

c. Permanent straightening effect

d. Enhanced hair color

Answer: a. Temporary straightening effect

Explanation: Keratin treatments provide a temporary straightening effect, typically lasting for several weeks.

What role does heat play in the process of chemical relaxers for hair straightening?

a. Enhances hair color

b. Activates the relaxing agent

c. Reduces processing time

d. Adds volume to the hair

Answer: b. Activates the relaxing agent

Explanation: Heat is often used to activate the relaxing agent in chemical relaxers, aiding in the straightening process.

Which hair straightening method involves the use of small, heated ceramic plates to straighten sections of hair?

a. Relaxer method

b. Thermal reconditioning

c. Keratin treatment

d. Flat iron method

Answer: d. Flat iron method

Explanation: The flat iron method involves using small, heated ceramic plates to straighten sections of hair.

What is the primary drawback of using chemical relaxers for hair straightening?

a. Long processing time

b. High cost

c. Risk of hair damage

d. Limited availability

Answer: c. Risk of hair damage

Explanation: Chemical relaxers can cause damage to the hair if not applied properly or if used excessively.

Which hair straightening method is known for its ability to maintain natural curl patterns while reducing frizz and enhancing shine?

a. Japanese straightening

b. Keratin treatment

c. Brazilian blowout

d. Chemical relaxer

Answer: b. Keratin treatment

Explanation: Keratin treatments are designed to reduce frizz and enhance shine while maintaining natural curl patterns to some extent.

What is the primary purpose of a Brazilian blowout in hair straightening?

a. Permanent straightening effect

b. Temporary straightening effect

c. Curling the hair

d. Reducing hair volume

Answer: b. Temporary straightening effect

Explanation: A Brazilian blowout provides a temporary straightening effect, typically lasting for a few weeks.

Which hair straightening method is also known as "thermal reconditioning"?

a. Keratin treatment

b. Brazilian blowout

c. Japanese straightening

d. Chemical relaxer

Answer: c. Japanese straightening

Explanation: Japanese straightening is often referred to as "thermal reconditioning" and involves permanently straightening the hair.

What is the primary ingredient in the solution used for Japanese straightening?

a. Sodium hydroxide

b. Formaldehyde

c. Keratin

d. Ammonium thioglycolate

Answer: b. Formaldehyde

Explanation: Japanese straightening solutions often contain formaldehyde, which helps in permanently altering the hair structure.

What type of hair is characterized by a smaller diameter and tends to be more delicate and prone to breakage?

a. Coarse hair

b. Fine hair

c. Thick hair

d. Frizzy hair

Answer: b. Fine hair

Explanation: Fine hair has a smaller diameter and is generally more delicate, making it prone to breakage.

How does color treatment affect the porosity of hair?

a. Increases porosity

b. Decreases porosity

c. No impact on porosity

d. Enhances thickness

Answer: a. Increases porosity

Explanation: Color treatment can increase the porosity of hair, making it more receptive to moisture but also more prone to damage.

What is a common concern for individuals with color-treated hair?

a. Reduced shine

b. Increased thickness

c. Enhanced elasticity

d. Reduced porosity

Answer: a. Reduced shine

Explanation: Color-treated hair can sometimes experience reduced shine as a result of chemical processing.

What precaution is advisable for fine hair to prevent breakage during styling?

a. Use a high-heat setting on styling tools

b. Apply heavy styling products

c. Minimize heat styling

d. Brush vigorously when wet

Answer: c. Minimize heat styling

Explanation: Fine hair is more prone to breakage, so minimizing heat styling can help prevent damage.

How can damaged hair be identified?

a. By increased elasticity

b. By a smooth, even texture

c. By a lack of split ends

d. By rough and brittle texture

Answer: d. By rough and brittle texture

Explanation: Damaged hair often has a rough and brittle texture, and it may show signs of split ends.

What is a suitable treatment for color-treated hair to maintain vibrancy?

a. Frequent heat styling

b. Sun exposure

c. Deep conditioning treatments

d. Brushing vigorously when wet

Answer: c. Deep conditioning treatments

Explanation: Deep conditioning treatments can help maintain the vibrancy of color-treated hair and improve its overall health.

How does the application of heat styling tools impact damaged hair?

a. Repairs damage

b. Reduces breakage

c. Worsens damage

d. Increases thickness

Answer: c. Worsens damage

Explanation: Excessive heat styling can worsen damage to already compromised hair, leading to further breakage and dryness.

What type of rod will achieve a wide and even wave formation when performing a permanent waving process?

a. Concave rod

b. Spiral rod

c. Straight rod

d. Body wave rod

Answer: a. Concave rod

Explanation: Concave rods are designed to create wide and even wave formations in hair during the permanent waving process. They produce a smooth, natural-looking wave pattern suitable for various hair lengths and textures. Large straight rod can also do the job.

What effect does blow drying hair with a round brush typically achieve?

a. Straightening hair

b. Aiding in curling the hair

c. Creating very tight curls

d. Minimizing frizz

Answer: b. Aiding in curling the hair

Explanation: Blow drying hair with a round brush helps to add volume and body by lifting the hair at the roots and creating a smooth, rounded shape. It is a common technique used to create fullness and bounce in hairstyles. Simply put, it aids in curling the hair.

How should the hair be cured after a chemical treatment, such as a perm or color treatment?

a. By immediately washing with cold water

b. By blow drying on high heat

c. By neutralizing or rinsing according to product instructions

d. By applying additional chemical treatments

Answer: c. By neutralizing or rinsing according to product instructions

Explanation: After a chemical treatment, such as a perm or color treatment, the hair should be cured by neutralizing or rinsing according to the product instructions. This process helps to stabilize the hair's pH balance and prevent damage.

What is the position in which the comb is held when tapering the hair with clippers?

a. Tilted away from the head

b. Perpendicular to the scalp

c. Diagonal to the scalp

d. Horizontally

Answer: a. Tilted away from the head

Explanation: When tapering the hair with clippers, the comb is typically held tilted away from the head to achieve a smooth and even blend between different hair lengths. This technique helps to create gradual transitions and precise cutting lines.

Which of the following rod types is best suited for creating tight curls in hair during a permanent waving process?

a. Concave rod

b. Spiral rod

c. Straight rod

d. Body wave rod

Answer: b. Spiral rod

Explanation: Spiral rods are designed to create tight curls in hair during the permanent waving process. They produce defined, spiral-shaped curls that are ideal for adding texture and volume to the hair.

What is the primary purpose of using a round brush when blow drying hair?

a. To create tight curls

b. To straighten the hair

c. To add volume and body

d. To minimize frizz

Answer: c. To add volume and body

Explanation: The primary purpose of using a round brush when blow drying hair is to add volume and body by lifting the hair at the roots and creating a smooth, rounded shape. It helps to achieve fullness and bounce in hairstyles.

What is the final step in curing the hair after a chemical treatment?

a. Blow drying

b. Neutralizing or rinsing

c. Applying a conditioning treatment

d. Cutting

Answer: b. Neutralizing or rinsing

Explanation: The final step in curing the hair after a chemical treatment, such as a perm or color treatment, is neutralizing or rinsing according to the product instructions. This step helps to stabilize the hair's pH balance and lock in the desired results.

How should the comb be positioned in relation to the scalp when tapering the hair with clippers?

a. Diagonally

b. Perpendicularly

c. Horizontally

d. Parallel

Answer: d. Parallel

Explanation: When tapering the hair with clippers, the comb should be positioned parallel to the scalp to achieve a smooth and even blend between different hair lengths. This technique helps to create precise cutting lines and gradual transitions.

Which rod type is typically used to create loose, natural-looking waves in hair during a permanent waving process?

a. Spiral rod

b. Concave rod

c. Straight rod

d. Body wave rod

Answer: d. Body wave rod

Explanation: Body wave rods are designed to create loose, natural-looking waves in hair during the permanent waving process. They produce soft, voluminous waves that add texture and movement to the hair.

What is a wet sanitizer used for in a salon setting?

a. Conditioning the hair

b. Styling wet hair

c. Sanitizing tools and equipment

d. Enhancing hair color

Answer: c. Sanitizing tools and equipment

Explanation: A wet sanitizer is used in salons to sanitize tools and equipment such as combs, scissors, and brushes to maintain cleanliness and prevent the spread of bacteria and infections.

What does a full bang style refer to in hairdressing?

a. Creating a layered haircut

b. Adding highlights to the hair

c. Styling the hair with bangs that cover the entire forehead

d. Using a specific technique to straighten the hair

Answer: c. Styling the hair with bangs that cover the entire forehead

Explanation: A full bang style involves cutting and styling the hair to create bangs that cover the entire forehead, providing a bold and dramatic look.

What test must be performed to determine the processing time for a chemical straightener?

a. Patch test

b. Elasticity test

c. Porosity test

d. Strand test

Answer: d. Strand test

Explanation: A strand test must be performed to determine the processing time for a chemical straightener. This involves applying the straightening product to a small section of hair to assess how long it takes for the desired result to be achieved.

Which color is added to neutralize a yellow tone in colored hair?

a. Blue

b. Red

c. Green

d. Purple

Answer: d. Purple

Explanation: Purple is added to neutralize a yellow tone in colored hair. This is because purple is the complementary color to yellow on the color wheel, and it helps to cancel out unwanted yellow hues.

When cutting an elevated bob, where does sectioning begin?

a. At the crown

b. At the nape

c. At the temples

d. At the bangs

Answer: b. At the nape

Explanation: When cutting an elevated bob, sectioning typically begins at the nape of the neck. This allows the stylist to create a solid foundation and build layers gradually towards the crown.

When cutting hair with medium graduation, at which angle must the hair be held?

a. 0 degrees

b. 45 degrees

c. 90 degrees

d. 180 degrees

Answer: b. 45 degrees

Explanation: When cutting hair with medium graduation, the hair is typically held at a 45-degree angle from the head. This angle helps to create a smooth, graduated effect with a moderate amount of layering.

What is the effect of a damp comb on thermally straightened hair?

a. Enhanced straightening

b. Reduced straightening

c. Increased curling

d. No effect

Answer: a. Enhanced straightening

Explanation: A damp comb can enhance the straightening effect on thermally straightened hair by providing moisture and tension to the hair strands, resulting in a sleeker and smoother finish.

What is a Thioglycolate relaxant commonly used for in hairdressing?

a. Adding volume to the hair

b. Creating curls or waves

c. Removing unwanted hair color

d. Strengthening the hair

Answer: b. Creating curls or waves

Explanation: Thioglycolate relaxants are commonly used in hairdressing to create curls or waves by breaking and reforming the disulfide bonds in the hair's protein structure, allowing the hair to take on a new shape.

When coloring hair, which volume of peroxide is required to lift a natural level 5 to a level 8?

a. 10-volume peroxide

b. 20-volume peroxide

c. 30-volume peroxide

d. 40-volume peroxide

Answer: c. 30-volume peroxide

Explanation: To lift a natural level 5 hair to a level 8, 30-volume peroxide is typically required. Higher volumes of peroxide are needed for greater lift, while lower volumes are suitable for less drastic color changes.

END OF BOOK

Manufactured by Amazon.ca
Acheson, AB